For all my kids,
Lucy, Phoebe and Pacific,
the new little healer growing inside of me,
and my niece and nephew Sovanna and Kosal.
I hope you always let your light shine.

Little Healers

Let Your Light Shine

Written by
Becky Payne

Illustrated by
Moran Reudor

"To Be the light"
is to be peaceful and
show others
Joy and Kindness.

This is Lucy.
She is the light.
You are the light.

This is Lucy's family. They are going to help show you how Lucy shines her light.

Lucy is the light because she trusts herself.

Lucy loves herself and others.

Lucy is caring.

Lucy expresses her feelings, even when she is sad or mad.

Lucy listens to other people.

Lucy takes care of herself and others.

Lucy lets her light shine.
The light is within you.
You are the light.

Shine brightly, little healer!

www.ingramcontent.com/pod-product-compliance
Lightning Source LLC
Chambersburg PA
CBHW050804220426
43209CB00089BA/1679